PAS[...] ON

Can you keep a secret?

I'm Lektron the robot and I'd like to welcome you to *Pass it on.* In this issue of *The Navigator* you'll find out more about different ways of communicating. Words aren't always necessary, you know! You'll be dotty about the top-secret report on Morse code, not to mention the article on secret messages. Pack your bags and prepare for some time travel as I whisk you away to a town in 2025, where robots like me play a part in making the streets a safer place for you humans.

Get cracking!

Text Type	Literacy Skills	Wider Curriculum Links
Reference	Language analysis; use of typography	**History** Units 14 and 15: Who were the Ancient Greeks? How do we use Ancient Greek ideas today?
Report	Summarising information; locating and interpreting information	**History** Unit 13: How has life in Britain changed since 1948?
Persuasive	Exploring authorial intent; expressing and justifying an opinion with reference to the text	**Design and Technology** Unit 5C: Moving toys
Report: Interview	Information retrieval; deductive comprehension; expressing and justifying an opinion with reference to the text	**Design and Technology** Unit 5A: Musical instruments
Report	Summarising information; deductive and inferential comprehension	**Science** Unit 5B: Life cycles
Report/ Recount/ Explanation	Information retrieval; deductive comprehension	
Report: Newspaper	Distinguishing between fact and opinion; expressing and justifying an opinion with reference to the text	**Geography** Unit 16: What's in the news?
Report/ Persuasive	Summarising information; inferential and deductive comprehension	**Geography** Unit 16: What's in the news?
Recount	Expressing and justifying an opinion with reference to the text	**PSHE:** Developing a healthier lifestyle; preparing to play an active role as citizens
Recount	Summarising information	
Fun spread		
		ICT: Year 5 Schemes of work

It's all Greek to me!

Can you speak Greek? No? Think again! Many everyday English words are derived from the language of ancient Greece.

Have a look at this picture to find out how many Greek words you really know!

conker *the shiny brown nut from a horse chestnut tree*
From *konkhe*, meaning 'shell'. The game of 'conkers' was originally played using snail shells.

aeroplane *a flying machine*
From *aer*, meaning 'air', + *planos*, meaning 'wandering'

alphabet *the characters used in a language, usually in a particular order*
From *alpha* + *beta*, the first two letters of the Greek alphabet

arachnophobia *fear of spiders*
From *arakhne*, meaning 'spider', + *phobia*, meaning 'fear'

architect *a person who designs buildings*
From *arkhi*, meaning 'chief', + *tekton*, meaning 'builder'

church *a place of worship for Christians*
From *kuriakon*, meaning 'house of the Lord'

crocodile *a large reptile*
From *krokodilos*, meaning 'worm of the stones'

dinosaur *a prehistoric animal*
From *deinos*, meaning 'terrible', + *sauros*, meaning 'lizard'

gargoyle *a carved stone face with exaggerated or distorted features*
From *gargarizein*, meaning 'to gargle'. Gargoyles are often used on buildings at the end of guttering. The word imitates the sound of water gurgling through the gutter.

hippopotamus *a large African animal which lives near water*
From *hippos*, meaning 'horse' + *potamos*, meaning 'river'

photograph *an image produced on light-sensitive paper*
From *photo*, meaning 'light', + *graphos*, meaning 'written'

telephone *a system which lets people speak to one another over distance*
From *tele*, meaning 'at a distance' or 'far off', + *phone*, meaning 'sound'

WHAT DOES IT MEAN?

Prefixes and suffixes that come from Greek are often used in English words. Knowing what these beginnings and endings mean can help us to work out the meanings of unfamiliar words.

Can you work out what these words mean, using the Greek words to help you?

- archangel
- archbishop
- arch-enemy
- asteroid
- astrology
- astronaut
- hydrophobia
- technology

PREFIXES AND SUFFIXES FROM GREEK

arch = 'chief'
astro = 'star'
hydro = 'water'
logy = 'the study or science of'
naut = 'sailor'
oid = 'shape'
phobia = 'fear'
tech = 'art or craft'

ANIMAL WELFARE

The leopard is just one animal still hunted for its fur.

For centuries, people have exploited animals for food, clothing, or entertainment. Gradually, however, we are learning to treat animals with more respect.

PROTECTING ANIMALS

The first ever anti-cruelty law was the Animal Protection Act, passed in 1822. Two years later, the Society for the Prevention of Cruelty to Animals (SPCA) was formed. When Queen Victoria granted it 'Royal' status in 1840, it became known as the RSPCA. It is the world's oldest animal welfare organisation. The RSPCA now handles 1.6 million calls and treats 280 000 animals every year. It also re-houses over 96 000 animals.

Today there are hundreds of organisations working to help animals. Some, like the Battersea Dogs' Home or the People's Dispensary for Sick Animals (PDSA), only look after sick, injured or unwanted animals. Others campaign for animal rights or take direct action to protest against animal cruelty.

RSPCA

The RSCPA has been working to improve animal welfare for more than 170 years.

BORN FREE FOUNDATION

The Born Free Foundation's 'Zoo Check' has improved the lives of many animals in captivity.

DURRELL WILDLIFE CONSERVATION TRUST
SAVING SPECIES WORLDWIDE

Workers at Jersey Zoo are dedicated to saving animals from extinction.

RESCUE WORKERS

Fifty years ago, many zoos were nothing more than animal prisons, where people came to stare at amazing creatures crammed into tiny cages. Today, organisations like the Born Free Foundation carry out 'health checks' to stop cruelty to zoo animals.

We now expect zoos to benefit the animals, not just entertain the visiting public. Jersey Zoo, founded in 1959 by naturalist Gerald Durrell, is a perfect example. It helps to save endangered species from extinction by breeding them in captivity and returning them to the wild.

PET PATROL

As pet ownership increases, new laws are needed to ensure that animals are well-treated. In 1983, the original Pet Animals Act (1951) was changed to give animals better protection. Nowadays, information and advice on pet care is much better than it used to be, and pet shops are inspected more carefully.

The demand for exotic pets like snakes, parrots and lizards has also increased. This has led to wild animals, including rare species, being trapped and sold illegally. Many die in the process. The Environmental Investigation Agency works 'under cover' to expose this illegal trade.

KEEPING UP THE PRESSURE

When celebrities protest against animal cruelty, people listen.

A French actress called Brigitte Bardot helped to save Arctic seal pups from being clubbed to death.

Fur coats were very fashionable until David Bailey, a famous photographer, produced an advert showing how many animals were slaughtered to make them.

Linda McCartney's vegetarian pre-prepared food and cookbooks persuaded many people to change their diet.

These days, some shoppers will only buy 'free-range' goods, because they believe that battery farming is cruel. Food labelling is helping consumers to choose more 'animal-friendly' products.

Exotic birds such as this toucan are taken from the wild and sold illegally.

Shoppers can now choose to buy 'dolphin-friendly' tuna fish.

THE FUTURE

Today, animals are still killed for their meat or skins, used for scientific experiments, hunted for sport, and kept as pets or exhibits, but views on animal welfare continue to change. In another 100 years, who knows what people will think about circuses, fox-hunting, vivisection, bullfighting, fishing, or even horse racing?

THE MEGA MONSTER TRUCK

Boy, what a truck!

This mega monster has a mega bonnet, under which is concealed the monster of all monsters. Release the bonnet and you release a scaled-down model of one of the world's largest motor engines. This twenty-seven-litre, twelve-cylinder, forty-eight-valve titanium imitation tells you why this truck is mega!

With a top speed of 30 kph, you'll be glad of the sleek suspension and the Bison Bull Bars, enabling you to withstand any imaginable impact.

Its realistic mud splashes and window cracks give this monster a 'don't mess with me' look.

Learn how to jump cars, buses and other toys with the free Stunt Book. Other accessories include a tree to drive over.

The Mega Monster Truck makes an impact even when standing still.

Price: £40

THE DIAMOND BEACH BUGGY

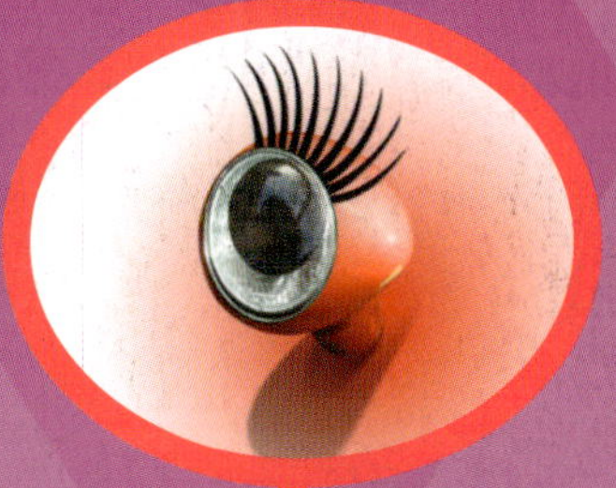

Are diamonds really a girl's best friend?

Well, this diamond comes complete with three detachable body panels in different colours, so the buggy will always co-ordinate your dress and mood, and an adjustable rear-view mirror which ensures easy make-up application.

The sun-roof dashboard-button allows you the luxury of watching the gentle-action soft-top go up and down, while avoiding unnecessary nail breaks.

And don't forget the other great accessories, such as the car wash and dashboard cleaning kit, the removable seat covers and floor mats, and the attachable headlamp eyelashes.

Altogether proving that diamonds really are a girl's best friend.

PRICE:
£40

Being a DJ

Have you ever been to a disco and danced until your feet hurt? If you have, then you'll know that while you were dancing, someone was working hard to make sure you were having fun. A DJ (short for Disc Jockey) chooses and plays the tunes that make your feet tap. DJ Michael McKenzie played his first disco (sometimes called a 'gig') when he was 12 years old. Quite a few years have gone by since then, but he still enjoys playing music to get you moving. He talks to our roving reporter, 10-year-old Katie Biggs.

Katie Biggs interviewing Michael

Living the dream

K: Did you always want to be a DJ?
M: Yes, DJ-ing was my dream, I thought it looked really cool … I had to be a DJ.

K: What's the first record you bought?
M: *Love don't live here any more* by Rose Royce, and my first album was by the Jackson Five.

K: What's your favourite type of music?
M: It's got to be 'Funky House' and fast music with a good beat.

Making people move

K: What's the best thing about being a DJ?
M: A DJ mixes music, making the music exciting and alive. I get a buzz out of getting people up, dancing and enjoying themselves. If they have had a good night, so have I.

K: What's the silliest dance you've ever seen?
M: The dance to the 'Birdy Song'.

K: Are you good at dancing?
M: That's a matter of opinion!

Michael at one of his gigs

Night owls

K: What time do DJs usually go to bed?
M: If I have a gig, I go to bed as late as 4 or 5 am. I sometimes have gigs that go on until 6 am, so I would be going to bed when you are getting up for school.

K: Do you sing in the shower?
M: No, I try not to, but it's a good place to sing!

K: Do you turn your music up really loud at home?
M: Sometimes, but the better the sound quality, the better the music, so you don't really need the music to be loud to enjoy it.

Hot stuff

K: Has anything ever gone badly wrong when you've been DJ-ing?
M: At a gig in the Wembley Conference Centre my equipment set off the fire alarm, which cut off the power – we had to evacuate the building!

K: Do DJs make lots of money?
M: If you're well-known or famous, you do.

K: Do you have any advice for children who'd like to be DJs?
M: Anyone who really loves music can be a DJ, if they work hard. Studying music is a good start and then on to a recording arts course to learn the technical bits. Whatever happens, **don't give up** – it really is worth it in the end!

Plants bite back!

Animals that eat plants are called herbivores. Eating a plant may sound easier than catching and killing an animal, but it is sometimes just as difficult or dangerous. Plants cannot run or hide, but they can still defend themselves. Some even eat animals!

What's in a name?

When a plant is dangerous, there is often a clue in its name. Only a fool would deliberately eat the berries of a deadly nightshade, try to pick a stinging nettle, or hug a prickly-pear cactus, but animals have to learn the hard way ...

The art of self-defence

Here are some examples of plants that are designed to put off hungry herbivores.

Even sharp thorns are no defence against a giraffe's tough mouth and sandpaper tongue

Look sharp!

- Thistles and holly bushes deter animals by growing prickly leaves. The long, stiff spines on a desert cactus help to protect the precious water stored in its trunk.
- African acacia trees have vicious thorns. Chewing a mouthful of acacia leaves must be like eating barbed wire, although giraffes don't seem to mind!

Keep off the grass

Have you ever wondered why a piece of grass is called a 'blade'? Every grass leaf is edged with a row of microscopic silica blades, like miniature glass swords, which wear away the teeth of grazing animals.

Poison arrows

- Stinging nettle leaves are covered in tiny needles. At the slightest touch, they break off and inject a small drop of poison. Animals avoid them, apart from caterpillars who can eat around the poisonous needles.
- The stinging trees in Australia are much more dangerous. Just brushing against their leaves can cause terrible pain that can last for weeks.

Bodyguards

Some plants have their own private army. They provide food and shelter for colonies of ants. In return, the ants guard the plant against leaf-eating insects. When plants and animals help each other in this way, scientists call it 'mutualism'.

Beware of the flesh-eaters!

Plants that grow on poor soil need to find extra nutrients. Some have solved this problem by eating meat ...

Soup of the day

Pitcher plants are named after the vase-shaped traps that sprout from their leaf tips. Attracted by sweet-smelling nectar, insects crawl down into the liquid-filled vase and drown in an acid soup that dissolves them into plant food.

The vase-shaped traps of the Pitcher plant lure unsuspecting insects into an acid soup

Meat sandwich

Each pair of hinged leaves on a Venus flytrap is covered in sensitive, trigger-like hairs. When an insect touches them, the leaves snap shut on their victim like the jaws of a hungry crocodile, and the plant's digestive juices go to work.

Many insects meet a sticky end between the jaw-like leaves of the Venus flytrap

The battle between plants and plant eaters is never-ending.

People's passions

Fancy being locked inside a block of ice, or bungee jumping off the Eiffel Tower? Or how about diving 150 metres under the sea on a single gulp of air? Someone has to do it ...

Queen of the Channel

"I don't think I will ever stop swimming the Channel. I'm addicted to it." (Alison Streeter)

Alison Streeter has swum the English Channel thirty-six times! When she was eighteen years old, she became the first woman to swim to France and back. Alison swims her fastest times when the sea is calm. But she gets her biggest adrenalin rush when there are obstacles to overcome – such as when she was cut by a boat propeller or attacked by stinging jellyfish. At the end of a swim, she feels exhausted – but her brain is on such a high, she always goes out to celebrate!

The Iceman

"People think I'm crazy but this is my way of challenging every human fear." (David Blaine)

In November 2000, magician David Blaine spent fifty-eight hours encased in ice in New York's Times Square. His body shape was cut into two blocks of ice which were then joined back together. A tube through the ice fed him oxygen and water. David practised by lying in a bath filled with ice. His record-breaking stunt was shown live on the Internet.

Champion free diver

"Our bodies possess incredible aquatic potentials. Some defy scientific explanation." (Pipin Ferreras)

In January 2000, Cuban-born Pipin Ferreras made a world record-breaking free dive off the coast of Mexico. Free diving is an extreme sport which can be very dangerous – divers dive as deep as they can on a single breath of air. They expose themselves to risks including blackouts, brain damage and sharks. Free divers can hold their breath for several minutes, using meditation techniques to lower their heart rate. Ferreras' dive lasted three minutes and twelve seconds, and reached a record-breaking depth of 162 metres.

Did you know?

Bungee-jumping was inspired by the vine jumpers of Pentecost Island in the Pacific Ocean. Each year, men from the island's tribes build huge wooden towers over 24 metres high. Then they throw themselves off the towers, tied to vines from the jungle. Modern bungee jumpers use latex rubber cord. A.J. Hackett opened the first jump to the public in New Zealand in 1987. He advertised it by bungee-jumping off the Eiffel Tower!

AND NOW for the NEWS...

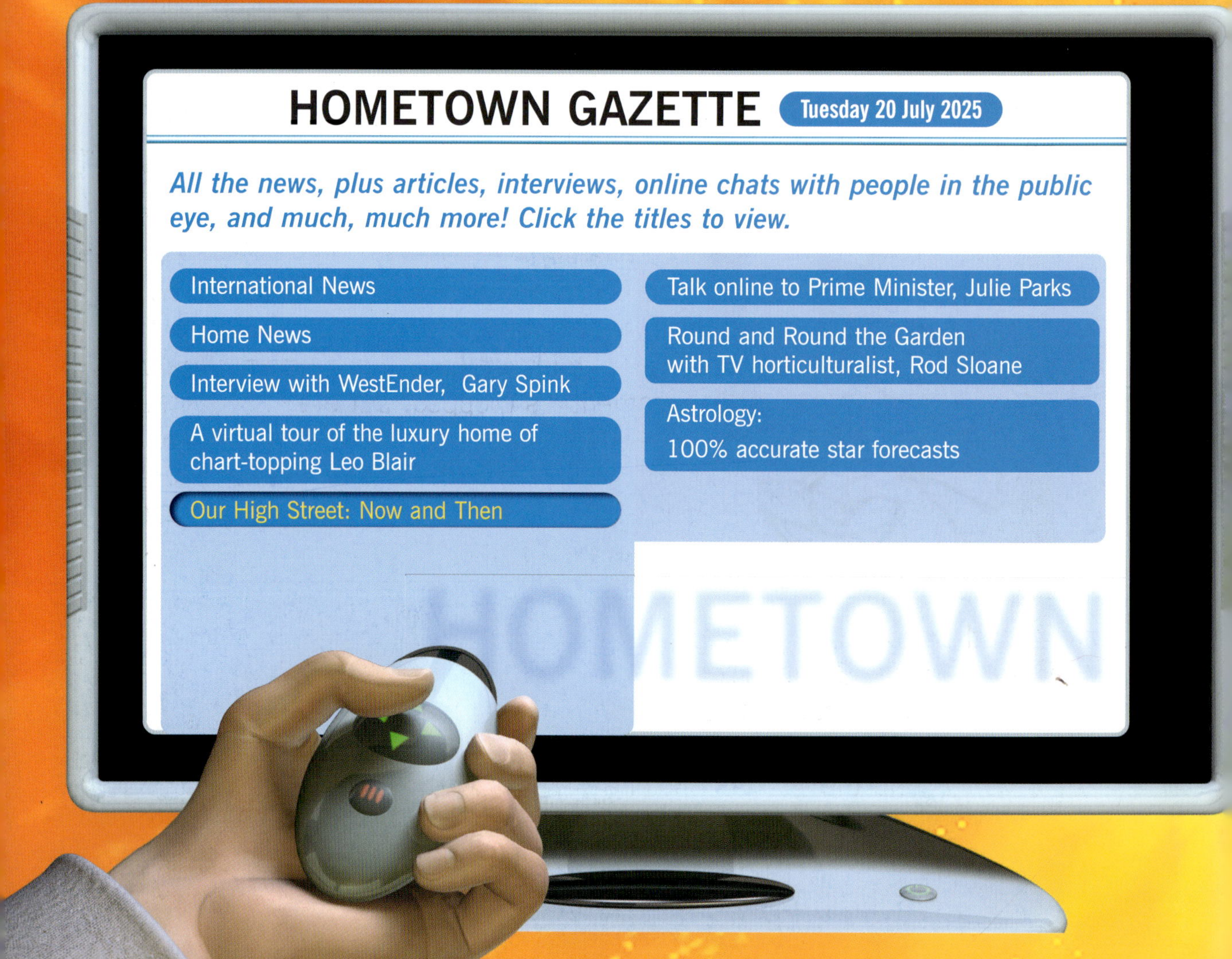

HOMETOWN GAZETTE

Tuesday 20 July 2025

All the news, plus articles, interviews, online chats with people in the public eye, and much, much more! Click the titles to view.

- International News
- Home News
- Interview with WestEnder, Gary Spink
- A virtual tour of the luxury home of chart-topping Leo Blair
- Our High Street: Now and Then
- Talk online to Prime Minister, Julie Parks
- Round and Round the Garden with TV horticulturalist, Rod Sloane
- Astrology: 100% accurate star forecasts

HOMETOWN

HOMETOWN HIGH STREET, 2025

Our High Street: Now and Then

Hometown's High Street today is a shoppers' paradise compared to the High Street of yesteryear. In 2025 we have the very latest **smoothway**, which carries us gently to the shops of our choice. In olden times pavements were poor, and roads weren't even **surfaced** to begin with. Later, many roads were **cobbled**. Then, until just a few years ago, they were covered in tarmac.

Until quite recently, dogs were allowed to foul the pavements. Unbelievable, isn't it? Today we have clean-up 'droids – **Whoopsies** – to clear the mess the moment it's dropped. But even Whoopsies will soon be a thing of the past, because live dogs are going to be banned from Hometown's streets. Clean, silent electric dogs – **Fidos** – are already proving very popular...

In the old days there were **muggers** and **pickpockets** everywhere. But in today's Hometown there are few opportunities for the baddies. Tiny hidden cameras are positioned all along our streets and the **Polbots** quickly apprehend felons. They deal just as efficiently with the occasional act of violence.

It amazes some people to learn that **traffic** was once permitted in town centres. The vehicles of 2025 are left in the car park that circles the town like a moat. Fast, free **Park & Ride Cablecars** carry shoppers and workers into town. There are no hold-ups, there's no traffic noise, no congestion or pollution – which means less stress for all of us.

Hometown's High Street is one of the most admired shopping centres in Europe. There's no litter; the **Litbugs** see to that. There's **soothing music** (musical link) wherever we go. We are protected from bad weather – in fact we don't even know if the **weather** is bad. How fortunate we are to live in these civilised times!

A LETTER TO THE EDITOR

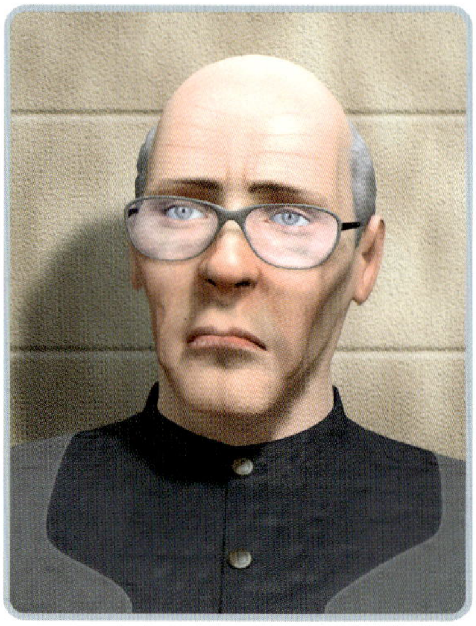

Sir. I have just read your article comparing today's High Street with the same environment of earlier days. Unlike many of your readers, I was born in the last century, and I have fond memories of life back then. While I appreciate that our ultra-safe society is superior in many ways, I feel obliged to point out to younger readers that there were advantages to living in those so-called 'unsophisticated days'.

I'm not referring to the excessive litter, or the traffic congestion and pollution. I'm not referring to the dog mess on the pavement. Nor am I referring to the muggings and the occasional street violence. When we went to the shops in my younger days we might have risked all sorts of things, but we were often surprised by something we saw or heard or experienced. Today there are no surprises. Everything is in its place. Everything is perfect. We are watched over every step of the way.

Well, I don't wish to be 'watched over'. Of course, I don't want to be mugged, or step in dog dirt, or be run over in the street. But I don't want to be mollycoddled either. There's so little to worry about these days, so little to anticipate, because everything is arranged and done for us. Without anticipation and worry, people stop using their imaginations. Their brains become dull. And that is the word I would use for this 'perfect' society of ours. Dull.

I for one am very bored with it.

Sincerely,

Hector Harbinger

PS. And will no one save me from that infernal music everywhere I go? We didn't have so much of that in my younger days, and very glad I was too!

NEWSFLASH

Lightning has struck the roof of the High Street Shopping Centre! Falling plastiglass has crushed the flowerbeds, and a number of people have been rushed to hospital. The lightning has also affected the central energy plant. Electricity has been cut off from many parts of town. These widespread cuts mean that robots and 'droids are incapacitated. Looters are running from shop to shop, loading stolen goods into hand carts, knowing that the polbots won't stop them and the hidden cameras won't be able to catch them on film.

We apologise to our readers, but the Gazette will also be affected soon, as will your home computers. If we still had access to printing presses (and paper) we might produce an old-fashioned version of your favourite newspaper as a temporary measure, but as things are we'll just have to wait until wi

BLACKOUT ▪ SHUTDOWN ▪ END OF BROADCAST

Which do you think you would prefer: life as we know it today, or a future like the one described in the Hometown Gazette? Which parts of each – present and future – would you keep?

Difficult dilemmas

TRICKY TRAFFIC

School is over for the day. Children stream through the school gates. Outside, there's a busy road. There are traffic lights and a crossing so that children can cross in safety, but today the lights aren't working. With the lights out of order, many of the cars don't stop to let the children cross. Children – and parents – take a chance and run over the crossing between vehicles.

Q ***What would you do in this dangerous situation?***

DON'T LOOK DOWN!

One Saturday morning, Oliver and Sarah are going to a nearby shop for their mother. They call "goodbye" to their dad, who is up a ladder cleaning the windows. Their dad looks down, and slips and falls. He lands safely in a big bush, but cuts his arm on the jagged branch of a tree on the way down.

Q ***What should Oliver and Sarah do?***

1: Call for an ambulance?
2: Call a neighbour?
3: Run for help?

Sensible solutions. But Sarah has an even better idea. She is one of the few children in her class who volunteered for First Aid training, so she knows exactly what to do!

NEIGHBOURHOOD WATCH

Katy knows that her new neighbours, Mr and Mrs Spiro, are away on holiday. One night, Katy hears a noise outside and looks out of her bedroom window. She sees a young man going round the side of the neighbours' house.

Q ***What would you do in Katy's position?***

What Katy does is ...

MORSE

If you've ever belonged to a secret club, you probably know what a code is. It is a way of altering a message to hide its real meaning. The person who gets the coded message uses a key to work it out.

A	.-	N	-.	1	.----
B	-...	O	---	2	..---
C	-.-.	P	.--.	3	...--
D	-..	Q	--.-	4	....-
E	.	R	.-.	5	.....
F	..-.	S	...	6	-....
G	--.	T	-	7	--...
H	....	U	..-	8	---..
I	..	V	...-	9	----.
J	.---	W	.--	0	-----
K	-.-	X	-..-		
L	.-..	Y	-.--		
M	--	Z	--..		

International Morse Code

Dots and dashes

In 1832, Samuel Morse thought of the idea for the electric telegraph while crossing the Atlantic Ocean on a ship. The telegraph was the first device to send messages by electricity.

At first, most telegraph messages were sent by tapping out a special code for each letter of the message with a telegraph key. The code, invented by Morse, used a system of 'dots' and 'dashes' to represent each letter of the alphabet, the numbers 1 to 9, and other symbols and punctuation marks. When tapping the code, a dash lasted three times as long as a dot. The telegraph changed the dots and dashes of this code into electrical impulses and transmitted them over telegraph wires.

Samuel Morse, is known as the father of the telegraph

SOS

After the ship Titanic sank in 1912, the International Maritime Organisation adopted SOS as the international distress (help) call. Some people think SOS means 'Save our Ship' or 'Save our Souls'. In fact it means neither. It was just decided that SOS in Morse code (... --- ... or 'dot, dot, dot, dash, dash, dash, dot, dot, dot') was easier to remember than the distress codes used previously.

CODE

Dotty about each other

Would you believe that the American inventor Thomas Edison used Morse code to propose to his second wife, Mina Miller? The two married in 1886. Thomas and Mina used Morse code to have secret conversations when her family was around. They tapped the code into each other's hands. One day Edison asked .-- --- ..- .-.. -.. -.-- --- ..-
-- .- .-. .-. -.-- -- . She answered -.-- . ...

Use the Morse code key to read what they said.

Thomas Edison and Mina Miller didn't need words to express their love to one another

Morse code rules OK!

Telegraph operators developed a shorthand for commonly used words and phrases in Morse code. The end of the message was code '30', meaning 'I have no more to send.' The code '73' meant 'Best wishes'. 'CQ' was a general call meaning 'Listen to this everyone!'. 'OK' was used from the 1840s onwards to mean 'All correct.' Now it is one of the most recognised words in the world.

Shhhhh...

Want to keep a secret? Use a code!

A code is any set of letters, words, colours, numbers or signs that has a special meaning. You can use the codes on these pages to send secret messages, or make up your own code that only you and your friends understand.

Pig Latin

To speak or write Pig Latin, take the first letter of a word and move it to the end, then add 'ay' (e.g. the word 'run'! becomes 'un-ray!'). If the word begins with two consonants, move them both to the end (e.g. 'write' becomes 'ite-wray'). If it begins with a vowel, leave the word as it is but add 'way' (e.g. 'ace!' becomes 'ace-way!').

What does this message say?

Ook-lay out-way! Eacher-tay in-way ight-say!

Txt-ing

Text messaging on mobile phones has led to a whole new language. You can shorten words by missing out vowels, such as writing 'gdlk' for 'good luck'. You can use numbers instead of letters – such as 'm8' for 'mate'. You can use letters that sound like whole words, such as 'C' for 'see', and 'R' for 'are.' So, 'See you later' becomes 'CUL8R'. 'Are you okay?' is written as 'RUOK?'

What does this message say?

U TLKING2ME? W8 4ME 2MORO NITE @ 7. DT B L8!

Pig pen cipher

Pig pen cipher has been used since the time of the Ancient Greeks and Romans! A cipher is a sign that stands for a letter of the alphabet. In Pig pen cipher, each letter is replaced with a symbol made up of straight lines and a dot. The language is based on a noughts and crosses board divided into nine "pig pens". Each pig pen contains three letters. Each letter is represented by the lines of its own pig pen, and its position in that pig pen.

A B C	D E F	G H I
J K L	M N O	P Q R
S T U	V W X	Y Z

For example: A =  P = 

What does this secret message in Pig pen cipher say?

The top secret Navigator code

You can use any symbol you like to represent a letter of the alphabet. Try using this Navigator code, known only to readers of 'The Navigator', to send secret messages to your friends.

Finally, try decoding this secret message in Navigator code.

Byte-Sized ICT

Being a DJ

Interview a star

Imagine that you had the chance to interview your favourite pop star or TV personality. What would you ask them? How their career began? What they do to chill out? Where they buy their clothes?

Using a word-processor, type out a list of the questions you would like to ask them. Don't forget the question marks!

You could also look on the Internet to see if your star has their own website. You may find the answers to some of your questions online. If you do, why not type in the answers to your interview questions? Set it out as if you were typing up a real interview, with initials to show who is speaking down the left-hand side, followed by a colon. You will have to imagine how they would say their answers.

Helpful hint!

If you save your questions, you can return to them at a later date and insert the answers by clicking after each question and pressing return to start a new line, then typing in your answer. You will also need to add your initials at the beginning of each question.

Animal welfare

ICT: Unit 5b: Using complex searches

Animal welfare research challenge

Use the Internet to find out more about a charity or organisation that helps to look after the welfare of animals. Can you find out three things they do, and three things you can do to help?

Remember, if you are using a search engine always include a couple of key words to focus your searches. Don't forget to use 'and' to keep your search narrow.

Helpful hint!

Charity websites usually have .org.uk at the end. You might find that they even have a section just for children.

Plants bite back!

Herbivore or carnivore?

Do you know your herbivores from your carnivores? Find out and then write a quiz to see if your friends can sort animals into the two different groups.

First you will need to do some research yourself, preferably using a CD-ROM. One that is just about animals will be most helpful. Remember, carnivores eat meat, herbivores eat plants. Make a list of animals, noting which are which, perhaps by putting H or C beside each. Most computers will allow you to use a word-processor at the same time as a CD-ROM, allowing you to type your list as you go. When your list is complete, copy and paste it into a new document and then delete every H and C. Ask a friend to type in which they think is which. Compare their answers with your list. Are they right?

People's passions

ICT: Unit 5f Monitoring

Icy water

What would happen to a block of ice left in your classroom for 58 hours? This is how long magician David Blaine spent encased in ice. In his case, the ice was kept frozen for all that time.

Place temperature sensor equipment in a pot containing some ice, and set it to measure the temperature at regular intervals over 58 hours. You will need to decide how frequently you want to know the temperature. Remember, you don't need temperature recordings every minute or you'll have far too much data!

You could try this using two or three different pots of ice, with different amounts of insulation. Which one will stay coolest longest? If 58 hours is just too long to wait, you could just try doing this over the course of one school day.

And now for the news…

The future's bright

How do you imagine the future? Will we all be riding around above the ground in helicars or cablecars? Will crime really be a thing of the past? Will teachers have been replaced by robots?

Prepare a presentation on your computer, using a multimedia or presentation program, showing your ideas of life in 2025. Try to include some sound effects and animated graphics if you can. You may be able to include links to take someone to different sections of your presentation by clicking on a word or picture.

Morse Code/Shhhhh...

Code-cracking capers

Sending messages in code can be great fun. Try typing out a message in Morse code, using full stops for dots and hyphens for dashes. Get a friend to decode it. You will need to leave a space between the code for each letter to make it clear. Use the chart on page 22 to help you.

Now try using a different code – perhaps Pig Latin or text messaging language. If you're feeling inventive, work with a friend to make up your own code. Try using some of the symbols on your computer to stand for different letters. If you decide to replace each letter with something different, type out a chart to remind you which symbol stands for which letter. Drawing a simple table with 26 rows (one for each letter) and two columns (one for the real letter and one for the code) will help you.

Real Letter	Code
a	*
b	
c	
etc.	

Glossary

adjustable its position can be changed

anticipate look forward to

apprehend arrest or seize

aquatic taking place in or on water

battery farming a method of farming that involves keeping hundreds of hens in a group of small cages and mechanically feeding them, to make them lay as many eggs as possible

civilised in an advanced state of society and culture

colony a group of the same kind of plants or animals that live close together

derive to come from a particular source

detachable can be taken off

deter discourage or prevent

exotic strikingly different and fascinating

exploit to use something or someone for your own advantage

extinction dying out completely, so none are left on the planet

felons villains, criminals

free-range produced by animals kept in natural conditions with the freedom to move about to look for food

horticulturalist a person who studies growing fruit, flowers and vegetables

illegally	against the law
infernal	unpleasant and annoying
looters	people who steal things during a battle or riot
mollycoddled	fussed over like a baby
nutrients	substances that give the energy needed for growth when they are eaten
prefix	a word part which is added at the beginning of a word to make a new word
printing presses	machines for printing books or newspapers
shorthand	a way of writing things down quickly using symbols instead of words
suffix	a word part which is added at the end of a word to make a new word
suspension	system of springs, etc., which support the body of a car over its wheels to absorb jolting and protect the car from damage
symbol	something that is used to suggest or stand for something else
tarmac	a mixture of tar and very small stones, used for making road surfaces
vivisection	using living animals in scientific experiments
volunteered	freely offered to do it
welfare	health and happiness

Index

For Angela, Amanda, Nina, Ella, Edward, Ella, Laurence, Archie and Coco
B.D.

For Soph and Jeff
T.H-N.

First published 1996 by Walker Books Ltd
87 Vauxhall Walk, London SE11 5HJ

This edition published 1997

10 9 8 7 6 5 4 3 2 1

This book has been typeset in Gill and Dinosaur.

Printed in Hong Kong

British Library Cataloguing in Publication Data
A catalogue record for this title is available from the British Library.

ISBN 0-7445-5233-8

When I Grow Up I WANT TO BE...

Written by
Blaise Douglas
Illustrated by
Tania Hurt-Newton

WALKER BOOKS
AND SUBSIDIARIES
LONDON • BOSTON • SYDNEY

When I grow up I want to be a

CHEF

That's for sure.

Yes! That's the perfect job for me
I should have thought of it before.
I'll grill lizard on toast
And stuff worms that I'll roast
With snake and asparagus tips.
I'll add my own pickled slugs
And lightly-boiled bugs,
And serve up the whole lot with chips.

On second thoughts…
That's a lot of washing up.

When I grow up I want to be a

MAGICIAN

That's for sure.

Yes! That's the perfect job for me
I should have thought of it before.
I'll do fabulous tricks
With cards, birds and bricks
And pull rabbits out of a hat.
I'll saw my assistant in half
Then just for a laugh
I'll go home and leave her like that.

On second thoughts…
It might all go horribly wrong.

When I grow up I want to be an

EXPLORER

That's for sure.

Yes! That's the perfect job for me
I should have thought of it before.
I'll sport a helmet and cane
And travel by plane,
Then by ship, then by camel or yak.
I'll cross Asia Minor,
Climb the mountains of China
And swim the Amazon on the way back.

On second thoughts...
I do get a little travel sick.

When I grow up I want to be a

MUSICIAN

That's for sure.

Yes! That's the perfect job for me
I should have thought of it before.
I'll play the flute and trombone
Drums, xylophone,
The banjo, piano and trumpet.
I'll blow and I'll drum,
I'll bang and I'll strum
And if the neighbours complain
They can lump it.

On second thoughts...
I may get a headache.

When I grow up I want to be a

VET

That's for sure.

Yes! That's the perfect job for me
I should have thought of it before.
I'll nurse sick dogs and cats
And cure short-sighted bats
And treat zebras
Who've come out in spots.
I'll make depressed hyenas giggle,
Teach eels how to wriggle
And undo pythons
Who've got tied in knots.

On second thoughts...
Animals can be very smelly.

B
N
G H

When I grow up I want to be a

FIRE-FIGHTER

That's for sure.

Yes! That's the perfect job for me
I should have thought of it before.
I'll climb ladders so tall
That if I were to fall
I'd be strawberry jam on the ground.
I'll fight fires with great ease
And rescue cats stuck in trees
Whenever the fire bell sounds.

On second thoughts...
I'm scared of heights.

When I grow up I want to be an

ASTRONAUT

That's for sure.

Yes! That's the perfect job for me
I should have thought of it before.
I'll call Mission Control
Then go out for a stroll,
Thousands of miles from the ground.
I'll eat what I wish
From a satellite dish.
I may even have dinner guests round.

On second thoughts...
I may get homesick.

When I grow up I want to be a

RACING DRIVER

That's for sure.

Yes! That's the perfect job for me
I should have thought of it before.
Tracks start where they end
With the occasional bend,
So there's no need to look at a map.
I'll race in France and Japan,
Drive as fast as I can
And do lap after lap after lap.

On second thoughts...
I may get dizzy.

2
6

When I grow up I want to be a

DEEP-SEA DIVER

That's for sure.

Yes! That's the perfect job for me
I should have thought of it before.
I'll harangue the herring
And bark at the shark
And wrestle the odd octopus.
Then I'll find an old wreck
And drink milkshakes on deck
With a catfish that calls herself Puss.

On second thoughts...
It's a bit wet down there.

When I grow up I want to be a

DETECTIVE

That's for sure.

Yes! That's the perfect job for me
I should have thought of it before.
In next to no time
I'll solve the crime
Of the missing gold bullion bar.
I'll follow the clues
And appear on the news
With the crook and the getaway car.

On second thoughts...
Criminals can be quite rough.

BANK

When I grow up I want to be a

FILM STAR

That's for sure.

Yes! That's the perfect job for me
I should have thought of it before.
I'll live in Beverly Hills
Where you never pay bills
And drive the most fabulous car.
I'll buy diamonds and mink,
I'll paint my house pink
And my pool will be shaped like a star.

On second thoughts...
It might get a bit boring.

Star
Journal

When I grow up I want to be an

INVENTOR

That's for sure.

Yes! That's the perfect job for me
I should have thought of it before.
I'll wear a white coat,
Grow a beard like a goat
And stick hundreds of pens in my pocket.
I'll make fuel out of prunes
And fly to Jupiter's moons
In my home-made prune-powered
space rocket.

On second thoughts...
There'll be a lot of homework.

When I grow up I want to be...
Well, the truth is I'm not sure.

I think it's best to wait and see
I should have realized that before.
I'm not in a hurry
So why should I worry
It's far too early to know.
I'm not sure what I'll be
But at least I'll be me...

So I'll lie back and wait till I grow.

Put a photo of yourself over this one and see what you want to be when you grow up!

MORE WALKER PAPERBACKS
For You to Enjoy

LOVE, YOUR BEAR PETE
by Dyan Sheldon/Tania Hurt-Newton

When Brenda leaves her teddy bear, Pete, on the bus she thinks he's lost for ever. But then postcards start to arrive from all over the world – from Pete!

"A story likely to appeal to many older pre-school children and infants." *The Junior Bookshelf*

0-7445-3630-8 £4.50

NO PROBLEM
by Eileen Browne/David Parkins

Mouse is sure she can put together Rat's construction kit – NO problem! But as she – and her friends – soon discover, it's not as simple as it seems! The book includes a cut-out model to make.

"A fascinating and vividly illustrated story." *Books For Your Children*

0-7445-3632-4 £4.99

LITTLE CHICKEN CHICKEN
by David Martin/Sue Heap

Everyone laughs at Little Chicken Chicken when she makes a tightrope out of a piece of string and says her black stones fell out of a thundercloud. But when lightning flashes and thunder shakes the ground, Little Chicken Chicken's magic goes down a storm!

"Dare to be different is the message of this uplifting tale about the triumph of the imagination." *The Independent*

0-7445-5236-2 £4.99